PORTRAITS OF THE BRITISH CINEMA

PORTRAITS
OF THE BRITISH CINEMA

60 GLORIOUS YEARS
1925 – 1985

John Russell Taylor and John Kobal

SALEM HOUSE
SALEM, NEW HAMPSHIRE

PHOTOGRAPHS FROM THE KOBAL COLLECTION

This book is dedicated to all the British film photographers: A.R.P. Studios, James Bacon, Cecil Beaton, Davis Boulton, George Cannons (Cannons of Hollywood), George Courtney Ward, Fred Daniels, Otto Dyar, Arthur Evans, Eric Gray, Annette Green, Norman Gryspeerdt, Norman Hargood, Raymond J. Hearne, David James, John Jay, Ian Jeayes, Janet Jevons, Clifford Kent, Patrick Lichfield, Sandra Lousada, Cornel Lucas, Wilfrid Newton, Ted Reed, Sasha, Cyril Stanborough, Charles Trigg, Tunbridge, Florence Vandamm, Hugo N. van Wadenoyen, Dorothy Wilding, Eric Wilkins, Laszlo Willinger, John Young – in appreciation of their work and in the hope of discovering more about them.

The authors would like to thank the following film companies both past and present without whom there would be no British cinema:
British International Pictures, Wardour Films Ltd, London Films, Warner Bros, Goodtimes, MGM, British Lion, Britannica, Conquest, Gaumont, British & Dominion, Mayflower, Gainsborough, General Film Distributors, Individual Pictures, Rank, The Archers, Herbert Wilcox, Two Cities, Sydney Box, Pinnacle, Gabriel Pascal, Ealing, Group Films, Maurice Cowan, Avon, Remus, Romulus, ABPC, Vic Films, ABP, Partisan, Columbia, United Artists, Proscenium, Brandywine, CCM, Horizon, 20th Century Fox, Universal, Woodfall, Anglo-Allied, Paramount, Oakhurst, Granada, Quintra, EMI, Eon.

The authors and publishers have tried their best, in the time and from the sources available to them, to trace the names of the photographers and credit them accordingly. They regret where this proved impossible and hope to put right any errors or omissions in any subsequent edition as the information becomes available.

Copyright © John Russell Taylor and John Kobal 1985

Published by Aurum Press Ltd, 33 Museum Street, London WC1A 1LD

First published in the United States by Salem House, 1986, a member of the Merrimack Publishers' Circle, Salem, New Hampshire 03079.

ISBN: 0 88162 151 X

Library of Congress Catalog Card Number: 85-61560

Designed by Neil H. Clitheroe

Phototypeset by Comproom, London

Printed in Singapore by Toppan Printing Co. (S) Pte. Ltd

CONTENTS

STARS AND STUDIOS	6
A NOTE ON PHOTOGRAPHERS	21
THE THIRTIES	29
THE FORTIES	61
THE FIFTIES	90
THE SIXTIES	123
MODERN TIMES	145
LIST OF STARS	160

STARS AND STUDIOS

American stars had faces; British stars had voices. Of course, it is not quite as simple as that, but there is enough truth in the saying to suggest an explanation of why there were so few real British stars before the coming of the talkies.

There were plenty of actors who played leading roles in British films, but even in the early twenties, whenever a British producer wanted a real star – that is, one whose presence in a film was alone enough to bring money into the box-office – he was likely to import someone with the glamorous aura of Hollywood already about him or her. This explains, for example, the prominence in Alfred Hitchcock's early career of American stars like Betty Compson, Virginia Valli and Nita Naldi, not to mention the irruption elsewhere of Mae Marsh, Dorothy Gish, Will Rogers and others. Even home-grown star material usually had to go to Hollywood to acquire a true star image: Ronald Colman and Clive Brook, for example, did not make the subtle but unmistakable transition from leading man to star until the American cinema got to work on them; and the same might almost be said of Ivor Novello, considering all the brouhaha about him as a possible rival to Valentino when he went to America to make *The White Rose* for D. W. Griffith in 1923. But though that probably helped – and certainly the next year he began for the first time to figure high up in the popularity polls of British film fans – he actually became a star in the true sense with a British film, *The Rat*, in 1925.

At that point, Novello was one of the two British stars in British films who really counted (the other was the charming comedienne Betty Balfour) and this was largely the doing, as one might expect, of a producer: the first producer in the British cinema to function very much the way American producers did, Michael Balcon. In all such cases chance must initially have played as big a part as careful plotting and planning, but the sign of the great producer is his ability to see what opportunities chance may be offering him and to take them. Balcon must certainly have had some notion of the possibilities inherent in casting Novello, already known on stage and screen, in a film version of his great success *The Rat*, a role specifically tailored for his particular looks, personality and (limited) acting abilities – as it should have been, since he wrote it himself in collaboration with the actress Constance Collier. But neither Balcon nor anyone else knew for sure that it would make Novello into the super male star of the British screen. And when it did, at least Balcon was able to recognize the special quality in the public's response and build on it, rushing a sequel, *The Triumph of the Rat*, into production at once, and then bringing his new star together with his new star director, Alfred Hitchcock, for two films, *The Lodger* and *Downhill*, which would set the seal on the success of both. From the start – *The Rat* was in fact only his sixth feature film as a producer – Balcon had the enviable, and in the silent British cinema very rare, ability to think in larger terms than just from film to film. He had, by instinct it seemed, a clear idea of promotion over a whole programme, allowing talents to develop and be tested and directed by the public, which was already perfectly capable of making known its likes and dislikes.

Betty Balfour's popularity came about equally by chance, and was promoted in a much more improvisatory fashion by her mentor, producer-director George

IVOR NOVELLO, *c.* 1925, photograph Sasha

Pearson. In his 1920 film *Nothing Else Matters*, Pearson tried out two very young actresses, Betty Balfour and Mabel Poulson, in subsidiary roles. The film was a roaring success with critics and public, and Betty Balfour, as a comical cockney maid, was particularly noticed. Pearson immediately went into production with another film, *Mary Finds the Gold*, with Betty Balfour promoted to the star role; and later in 1921 he hit absolutely right with *Squibs*, in which the sort of bouncy, cheeky, effervescent character Betty Balfour had played in *Nothing Else Matters* was made the centre of the story. So successful was this that it was followed by a series of three more Squibs films, ending with *Squibs' Honeymoon* (1924).

By this time Betty Balfour was established as the only female British star to figure among the international poll-winners in Britain, and indeed quite simply as the only female British star. When she moved away from playing comical skivvies to slightly more sophisticated roles, the public followed her quite happily (she too passed through Hitchcock's hands in *Champagne*), and her popularity lasted well into the thirties: she even did a talkie remake of *Squibs* in 1935. Though Pearson was nowhere near the same class as Balcon in his production thinking, he had the sense, since Betty Balfour was his main asset, to exploit her special qualities by giving her plenty of opportunities to do what she could do best.

But then, both Ivor Novello and Betty Balfour had faces. Novello was famed far and wide (to his own embarrassment) as 'the most handsome man in England', and his profile was almost as celebrated as John Barrymore's. Though he had considerable experience, and success, on the stage, no one thought him the most wonderfully varied of actors. He usually did on stage what Hollywood stars did on screen: showed off the way he looked and with it a certain ebullient, boyish quality in his own personality. It just so happened that the camera also picked up and magnified these qualities, so that, given the proper vehicles, he could be a true film star – no doubt more satisfactorily than more gifted stage actors with a lot of theatre technique to get in the way.

It may seem odd, since Novello was so famous as a theatre matinee idol, and later as the composer and star of romantic musicals, to say that he had a face rather than a voice. But people forget that he himself never sang in his shows (he had, said Noël Coward, 'the sort of screechy off-pitch voice song-writers usually seem to have'), and it was in his voice that his limitations as a performer were most clearly apparent – the proof, if any be needed, lying in his failure to shine in talkies, where his over-refined and actorly diction cancelled out his charm and made him seem curiously antiquated.

Betty Balfour's film face was, naturally, rather a different matter: in this case, one suspects, it was an advantage that she began directly in films, at the age of 18, without any significant stage experience, for her mobility of feature, her gift of conveying mood and meaning with her eyes and expression in close-up, mark her off immediately from the other English leading ladies of the time, who were liable, however carefully they were directed, to do too much, emote from a distance destructive to the cinema's intimacy of effect.

The consistency of presentation, the effect of a career strategy (including appropriate publicity) which only a studio, or at least a producer, could achieve, was invaluable for both Ivor Novello and Betty Balfour. Though they had producers behind them, it was too early in the development of British cinema to say they had studios in anything like the sense already current in Hollywood. Indeed, even in the basic physical sense of bricks and mortar most of the British film studios were yet to come. There were dozens of tiny ones which came and went by the early twenties, the two most notable which survived from before 1914 being Teddington and Shepherd's Bush. The latter (now the BBC Lime Grove Studios) was overhauled and vastly expanded in 1926, at around the same time that the British International Studios at Elstree were being built. Most of the major British studios dated from the booms which alternated with busts throughout the thirties: Denham in 1934, Shepperton 1935, Pinewood 1936 and Amalgamated, later MGM, at Elstree in 1937 – and, very quietly and modestly, Ealing in 1931.

But most of these for most of their existence were simply places where films were made, not the integrated, monolithic structures of the famous Hollywood studios. If films had any corporate identity in the public mind, it was almost always that of the production company, which might be making its films anywhere for all picturegoers knew or cared to the contrary. The only exception to this rule was Balcon's management of Ealing between 1938 and 1956, where the name of the company and that of the studios coincided (films made elsewhere by Balcon continued to carry the Ealing label until 1959); in practice Korda ran his London Films at Denham in the thirties and Shepperton after the war as Hollywood-style operations, and J. Arthur Rank built his film-making activities at Pinewood along similar lines from very small beginnings in 1936 up to the heyday (from our point of view) of the Rank Charm School and the line-up of contract players and technicians in the period immediately after 1945.

That is to anticipate. When sound hit the British cinema in 1929 there was still lacking that sense of overall strategy which could make capable performers into film stars proper. Up to 1927 at least, the British film business had been a cottage industry, living very much from hand to mouth. The Quota Act of 1927 was much complained about, then and since, for its encouragement of the lowest form of British film, the 'quota quickie', which did the barest minimum to qualify as a British feature film and thus benefit from the protection of the Act which required a certain proportion of the films shown in British cinemas to be British made. But the Act did provide a firm basis for the rapid expansion and consolidation of British cinema: it offered a chance which was rapidly taken, even with the manifold confusions of the change-over to talkies, heralded most notably by Hitchcock's '99 per cent talkie' *Blackmail* in June 1929.

The company *Blackmail* was made for, British International Pictures (BIP) was the largest and most important to arise in the twenties; if not necessarily the most creative, it was certainly the nearest to a classic American company in its outlook. Founded by John Maxwell, a Glasgow lawyer, in 1926, it went public and acquired its name in 1927 and instantly set about a large-scale production programme based on its own newly expanded studios at Shepherd's Bush. At first it was less interested in building talents and reputations than in establishing sheer bulk of release and a regular flow to the cinemas. With this in mind the company signed up as many established figures as possible, including two refugees from Balcon's smaller Gainsborough company, the producer-director Victor Saville and directorial wunderkind Alfred Hitchcock. This rather *ad hoc* approach to building a company meant that there was not for some time, if ever, an observable consistency in BIP films. On the other hand, the heterogeneous product was, for the first time in the history of the British cinema, sold with some sort of consistency. Moreover, most of the films, though from a collection of semi-independent producers, were made together at Shepherd's Bush, backed by a studio organization which could, once it got the hang of such things, market its stars along with its other product in such a way that a public following might be built up.

BIP was very conscious of the visual angle. It was widely remarked that the first way in which the company's modernization of British film-making, along big-business lines, made itself apparent was in the look of the films, which, whatever their other qualities, had certainly lost the skimped and tatty appearance characteristic of most British films in the silent era. Camerawork on BIP films was of a uniformly high order. The company already had under contract one of the best British cameramen, J. J. Cox, and they proceeded to import Charles Rosher and René Guissart from Hollywood to show how it should be done, as well as pursuing the connections already established by Balcon with Germany, bringing in German cameramen such as Werner Brandes, Karl Püth and Theodor Sparkhul. With this went a far greater care in the selection of stills and star portraits for spreading the image along with the word in fan magazines. As yet the stills photographers remained an anonymous breed, minor functionaries of the studios, but at least the uses of their product had been recognized.

The establishment of the talkie in Britain brought some important new figures, with new ideas, into the British film business. The most spectacular of them, in every way, was a dynamic and devious Hungarian, Alexander Korda. Korda arrived in 1931, after working as a director first in Hungary, then in Austria and Germany (many of his films starred his tempestuous first wife Maria Corda, including two he made in Germany in 1926, *Madame Wants No Children* and *A Modern DuBarry*, which featured a young German actress, later to reach world-fame in Hollywood, Marlene Dietrich). From there he went to America in 1927, working for First National and Fox in Hollywood and, with the coming of sound, for Paramount in France. His first British picture, *Service for Ladies* (1932), was made for Paramount release. It starred the British actor Leslie Howard, who had become a film star in Hollywood, in his first British talkie. The film's female leads, Elizabeth Allen and Benita Hume, were both signed up by MGM on the strength of their showing in Korda's film. Korda was something of an entrepreneur, and looking around England, seeing the competition and sensing an opportunity and freedom he hadn't found elsewhere, he found his home. Almost at once he set up his own company, London Films, and proceeded to produce and direct for it two relatively modest films, *Wedding Rehearsal* and *The Private Life of Henry VIII*. The latter went on to become a phenomenal success in Britain and also in the United States, thus fulfilling the long-standing dream of British film-makers to challenge Hollywood on its own ground; its star, Charles Laughton, even won the all-important Hollywood Academy Award for his performance. On this basis, plus a lot of personal charm and business plausibility, Korda launched out as the dominating figure of thirties' cinema in Britain, developing his own company along Hollywood lines and building his own modern studios at Denham to house it.

Unfortunately Korda did not understand – or possibly scorned – the side of the Hollywood studio system which churned out B-features and bread-and-butter A's to keep the machine constantly working at full capacity and feed the theatres with a regular diet: too much money was spent on too few major, prestige productions, where one or two flops could prove totally disastrous. (As it proved with *Knight Without Armour*, a box-office failure for which Korda imported Marlene Dietrich from Hollywood at the then staggering salary of $450,000, and the collapse of the costly *I, Claudius*.) But at least he understood better than anyone else in Britain at that time the prime importance of making stars and then safe-guarding and polishing their image through a succession of the right roles in the right films, plus a constant back-up barrage of publicity. Thus Korda's major films of the thirties always star stars – people we would recognize even today as such, like Douglas Fairbanks, Sr (on his last go-round, admittedly, in *The Private Life of Don Juan*), Charles Laughton, Elisabeth Bergner, Leslie Howard, Paul Robeson, Raymond Massey, Laurence Olivier, Roland Young, Marlene Dietrich, Conrad Veidt, and many others. Not to mention the stars Korda invented and/or helped to build, like Merle Oberon, Binnie Barnes, June Duprez, Wendy Barry, Robert Donat, Vivien Leigh, Flora Robson and Sabu. Clearly he had no particular principles about the Britishness of his stars – even a number of those who were British in origin, like Leslie Howard and Roland Young, he happily exploited after Hollywood had done the spadework. But Korda did have proper ideas about how to use stars, and the studio organization to back them up.

In a much more modest way, Michael Balcon continued along his own line throughout the thirties. After running his own company, Gainsborough Pictures, he went in 1931 to be head of production for a larger concern, Gaumont-British. In 1936 he became head of production for the short-lived MGM-British company, but parted company with them after only one film (*A Yank at Oxford*) and took over direction of a smaller group which in 1939 assumed the name of its new home, Ealing Studios. Balcon had something of a reputation as a star-maker, justified no doubt by his having known how to develop Ivor Novello in the twenties. Later on, during the Ealing days, he was actually hostile to the whole idea of the star as centre of a film, but when he had any stars at all, he seems to have concentrated on one at a time and mostly taken them over from other producers as a painful necessity rather than fostering his own. The great star of Balcon productions in the thirties was Jessie Matthews, but her development seems to have owed more, in the vital early stages, to her regular director Victor Saville than to her producer. In general Balcon was quite content to adopt leading players from the stage and rely on their already existing popularity to carry them through, looking down rather puritanically on the publicity machines of bigger companies.

The two most closely comparable independent producers disagreed with him in this. Herbert Wilcox was a film-man from way back, who, after importing various American stars in silent days happened to strike lucky, personally and professionally, when he encountered one of Charles B. Cochran's 'young ladies' (a

BETTY BALFOUR, 1927, photograph James Bacon

MABEL POULTON, c. 1925

CLIVE BROOK, photograph Florence Vandamm

RONALD COLMAN, 1922,
photograph Hugo N. van Wadenoyen

particularly refined breed of chorus-girl) called Anna Neagle, who became his regular star and collaborator after *Goodnight Vienna* in 1932. Since from then on they rarely worked apart, he had little time to make any more stars, though he did invent a surprisingly satisfactory romantic duo after the war by combining Anna Neagle with Michael Wilding, until then a performer of very minor distinction. Basil Dean, an important stage director of famously savage temperament who took to the cinema in the late twenties, was on the contrary quite deliberately a star-maker. He had to his credit the screen careers of Gracie Fields and George Formby, the biggest of all working-class screen stars during the thirties, as well as that of his wife Canadian-born Victoria Hopper. Dean created Ealing studios originally as the home of his company Associated Talking Pictures.

What were these new British stars of the thirties like? How, if at all, were they distinguished from the Hollywood stars they were set to rival, and how, if at all, did they continue to stand out if they ever got to Hollywood? The secret, to come back to our initial over-simplification, always seems to be in the voice. The voices, of course, were not invariably those refined, upper-class tones that Americans like to imagine English actors are graced with: Gracie Fields and George Formby made their careers largely out of their North Country, working-class origins and their ability to stay always close to the people, which was principally expressed in the way they spoke and sang. Nor, perhaps, were the voices of the British stars, taken one by one, necessarily any more important than those of the equivalent generation of American stars who came to the fore with the talkie. Who ever forgets, for example, the sound of Bette Davis's voice, or Barbara Stanwyck's, or James Cagney's or Humphrey Bogart's?

And yet it has always been easier for people in America to make it straight to stardom from manning the gas pump or waiting at table, just on the way they looked and moved and photographed, than it ever was in Britain, where amazingly few have made it to fame without any training at all. It is as though, training and stage experience or no, the British film star is automatically more verbally orientated, and whether playing grand or common, always has to know how to do it with the voice as much as, if not more than, the look. It is hard to say whether this contributed significantly to the paucity of pre-talkie stars in Britain – especially considering they had so many other strikes against them in the amateurish way they were used – but it does seem that when they were given the freedom to speak for themselves they were able for the first time truly to expand and fill the screen. Their faces took on life.

Towards the end of the thirties a new force in British films began to emerge, the Northern flour tycoon J. Arthur Rank. He began in a small and decidedly unpromising way, as a man with a mission: he was a devout Methodist and started by promoting strictly religious productions. In 1935 he bought into a smallish company, British National, and began production modestly enough with an unpretentious drama of rival fishing fleets, *The Turn of the Tide*, shot largely on location. During its making Rank observed that film-making in a very small studio was uneconomical, and so conceived the idea of constructing a large modern studio, Pinewood. Things somehow naturally developed from there. Well, 'naturally' in the ways natural to the very rich who are not used to being crossed: when Rank had difficulty getting *The Turn of the Tide* distributed, he bought his way into a distributor; when he found fault with the studio system he built himself a studio, and by 1939 had controlling interests in Denham (Korda's financial bubble having burst by then) and Amalgamated's new, unused studio at Elstree; and when he realized that he also needed a theatrical outlet for his films if he was going to secure the whole operation, he bought his way also into the Odeon circuit of more than 200 cinemas, built up by a Birmingham scrap metal magnate called Oscar Deutsch during the thirties. (The Odeons, incidentally, were a unique example of physical image-building in the British cinema, all, or nearly all, being given the same name and built to the same recognizable pattern, to encourage immediate audience identification.)

And all this activity on Rank's part with scarcely any product as yet to justify it: either he was working from pique, or pragmatically as he saw holes in the system and business possibilities, or according to a long-term strategy bolder and more thought out than any other in the history of British films. Or possibly a bit of all three. Rank's biographer Alan Wood compares the Rank empire with the British Empire, allegedly acquired in a fit of absent-mindedness, and speaks of the 'apparently fortuitous, haphazard and higgledy-piggledy nature' of Rank's growth. There may also have been, who knows, an element of the 'call to greatness' about it: in the early days of the Second World War Korda had gone to America, John Maxwell of Gaumont-British died, and no other conceivable saviour of the British cinema was visible. If it was going to continue in production on any scale at all, it could only be through the intervention of J. Arthur Rank. Intervene he did, and things moved rapidly. In 1941 Rank took over Gaumont-British with its subsidiary companies such as Gainsborough Pictures; in 1941 he bought complete control of the Odeon circuit following the death of Oscar Deutsch; and in 1944 he bought out the other major interests in Pinewood and Denham studios to assume complete control of them. And all of this without denting his freely admitted ignorance of film-making: he put up the money and gave total scope to the creativity of the producers and directors who worked for him – with results sometimes disastrous, sometimes triumphant.

This way, naturally, all the most important film-makers in Britain gravitated to Rank with their projects; this way he acquired Laurence Olivier and his Shakespeare films, the products of the Archers (Michael Powell and Emeric Pressburger), the Cineguild group (which brought most significantly David Lean with his Noël Coward and Dickens films) and many more at the cultural end of the scale, including finally, in 1947, Rank's one-time arch enemy Michael Balcon and his operation at Ealing. But also, and as far as sheer showbiz values and star-building were concerned most important, there was the unashamedly populist production of Gainsborough Pictures, which provided most of the biggest stars and the biggest commercial successes of the war years and contributed enormously to the prosperity and even viability of Rank's distribution organization General Film Distributors (GFD).

From the point of view of image-making in the British cinema, it is worth looking at Gainsborough in a bit more detail. Founded by Balcon in 1924, in 1931 it became part of a larger group, Gaumont-British, when Balcon was appointed head of production there, with general charge of the studios at Shepherd's Bush as well as his smaller original enterprise in Islington. When in 1936 he left to head

MGM's British production programme, Gainsborough remained in the Gaumont-British fold, under the general control of the Ostrer family but more specifically in the charge of the young Tyneside show business veteran, Ted Black, brother of the theatrical impresario George Black. Black believed in the importance of the script – Gainsborough was the only British company that had a regular scenario department along Hollywood lines – the importance of the director – he was responsible for bringing on Carol Reed and produced his first big success, *Bank Holiday*, in 1938 – and above all, the importance of the star. He not only discovered and put under contract players like Margaret Lockwood, in whom he sensed a quality 'with which every girl in the suburbs can identify herself', building them up with the right roles and the right presentation to the public by the necessary spate of pictures and publicity, but he also saw the starring potential in such very different figures as the abrasive comedian Will Hay, and masterminded the series of vehicles which made him one of the most popular characters in the British cinema.

In the dicey days for British films at the beginning of the war Black moved his whole operation to Twentieth Century-Fox's British set-up, but when Rank emerged as a potential buyer for Gaumont-British, including Gainsborough, he was back there and ready for action. He rapidly extended his family of contract artistes to include, as well as Margaret Lockwood, James Mason, Phyllis Calvert, a handsome newcomer born James Stewart but rapidly rechristened for obvious professional reasons Stewart Granger, Jean Kent (a second-string Margaret Lockwood), Patricia Roc and many more. In 1943 the group hit jackpot with a piece of ripe costume tushery called *The Man in Grey*, starring Lockwood, Mason, Calvert and Granger in what were to become their characteristic roles, and when this was followed up in 1945 with *The Wicked Lady* (Lockwood and Mason again, with Patricia Roc and Griffith Jones in support) the pattern was perfected: Lockwood and Mason romped away with the first *Daily Mail* National Film Awards in 1946 as the most popular British stars of the time, and *The Man in Grey* was just pipped at the post as the most popular film by Anthony Asquith's 1945 wartime morale-booster, *The Way to the Stars* (which served to make audiences take notice of a strikingly beautiful brunette teenager named Jean Simmons).

Ironically enough, the war years were, partly despite and partly because of all the shortages and restrictions, a very good time for British films and British stars – the best, many would say. The relative shortage of competing foreign product, plus a certain sense of national beleaguerment and the patriotic duty to buy British, meant that for about the only time in its history the British cinema was actually the most popular with British audiences. The solid and reliable basis of commercial viability meant that a programme of classier, riskier enterprises could be built upon it. Both for popular entertainment and for quality product more likely to appeal to critics and minority audiences, the prospects had never been more favourable. After the war things changed as tastes changed and British cinemas were again flooded with American product, even as the pursuit of the crock of gold represented by a chimerical American market became again practical for British film-makers, if no more than ever likely to succeed. American stars (Paulette Goddard, Myrna Loy, Kim Hunter, Orson Welles) were again brought over to Britain, and British stars (Phyllis Calvert, Patricia Roc, Ann Todd) were shipped to Hollywood for one or two films at a time in a pathetic approximation of lease-lend, and Rank enterprises found themselves involved in such costly disasters as Gabriel Pascal's leaden version of Shaw's *Caesar and Cleopatra* (1945, starring the Hollywood-crowned Vivien Leigh) and the heavyweight imitation Hollywood musical *London Town* which was expected to make a star of newcomer Kay Kendall but set her career back by ten years, both made primarily for an American market which predictably failed to materialize since the Hollywood studios were not about to give an inch of their territory to outsiders, regardless of sharing a common language.

Meanwhile at home change was in the air. Margaret Lockwood, James Mason and reckless Regency costume romance were supplanted in the popularity tables by Anna Neagle and Michael Wilding in the glossy but more serious-seeming inventions of Herbert Wilcox, back from America and back in business again with Associated-British and other Rank rivals, turning out such contemporary stories as *Piccadilly Incident* and *Spring in Park Lane* and inspirational period pieces like *The Lady with the Lamp,* in which Anna Neagle as Florence Nightingale was able to continue her impersonation of heroines of British history, with which she had made her reputation in the thirties as Nell Gwynn and Queen Victoria. Rank was in trouble; the British cinema in general was in trouble; and in 1948-9 the whole business plunged into a major crisis, which entailed a lot of retrenchment by Rank and, surprisingly enough, the reappearance of Alexander Korda as the new saviour, this time with government backing through the National Film Finance Company.

As it happened, Korda had been building up to this for some years. He had come back from Hollywood during the war with just a producer-director arrangement with MGM, out of which one film emerged, *Perfect Strangers*, starring Robert Donat and Deborah Kerr. But by skilfully reissuing his old films he managed to refloat his old company, London Films, to buy a controlling interest in the British Lion distribution company, to purchase Shepperton Studios and the smaller studios at Isleworth, and then to take over a lavish mansion in Piccadilly as his centre of operations, as well as the Rialto Cinema as his own West End showcase. He had also managed to lure over from Rank (in 1945) Edward Black and his prize director Leslie Arliss, and he started production, in a modest way, with three low-budget films by associated producers to begin a steady flow through his studios and to the cinemas. As the Korda group grew in strength, and Rank felt more and more the breezes of crisis-time, the trickle of talent from Rank to Korda became a flood: in rapid succession came Carol Reed (*The Third Man*), David Lean (*The Sound Barrier*), Powell and Pressburger (*Tales of Hoffman*), Launder and Gilliatt (*The Happiest Days of Your Life*), and Laurence Olivier, whose *Richard III* was one of the last films produced by Korda's company in 1956.

Whereas Rank was the great non-interferer with his film-makers, Korda was very determinedly the movie tycoon, American model. Also, sometimes disastrously, the film-maker and frustrated film-maker who could not resist imposing his frustrations along with his authority on some of his more vulnerable tributaries. By now he seemed to be past making stars – perhaps because of his

The fisheries, Denham

Rank's Pinewood Studios

British International Pictures, Elstree, 1957

Warner Studios, Teddington: main entrance and offices, 1938

Shepperton Studios, 1958

long personal disillusionment with his very own invention Merle Oberon (in a repetition of the error of his ways with former wife Maria), Trilby to his Svengali, whom he brought to stardom in 1933, married in 1939 and finally divorced in June 1945. Rank, even in his depleted state, was (creatively as well as legally) still backing the build-up on popular fifties attractions like Dirk Bogarde, Laurence Harvey, Anthony Steel and Michael Craig, while the feminine angle was taken care of, partly by Rank, partly by smaller companies like Associated British, with such as Diana Dors, Kay Kendall and Joan Collins. Most of the new British stars who did emerge were snapped up by Hollywood, temporarily (Anne Crawford, Richard Todd, Joan Rice) or permanently (Deborah Kerr, Audrey Hepburn, Claire Bloom), and those who remained at home quickly faded from the screen or slid gracefully into character roles. The traffic the other way was also for a while intense: on the supposition, misguided as it proved, that the mere presence of an American name in an allegedly British film would ensure it an audience on the other side of the Atlantic, lots of – usually falling – stars were brought over to decorate 'mid-Atlantic' productions, thereby doing no good to themselves or anybody else.

By the time Korda died at the beginning of 1956, he had already run through his big spending spree, produced some of the best British films of the early fifties, and lost most of his major assets, including British Lion. But times were changing again, faster than anyone comprehended. Prophetically, one of Korda's last projects was a plan to enter television production, though even he probably did not realize how urgently the new medium was treading on the heels of the traditional movies. Even in Hollywood the old studio system of contract stars and year-round production with a large permanent staff was beginning to break down. More and more stars wanted to be independent, and fewer and fewer studios, after the divorce of distribution and exhibition enforced by the anti-trust laws (companies were no longer allowed to block-book their own films into their own cinemas), could afford to keep up production on the old, grand factory-scale. From then on, despite occasional valiant attempts to reverse this trend, it has been every man for himself in the British cinema, with 'stars' as an international commodity, marketed in much the same way as anyone else who, for a day or a week, is just famous for being famous. Essentially the public now decides, as it always really has done, exactly whom it is interested in and whom not. The only thing is that now fame and the ability to sell newspapers and magazines on the power of a name do not necessarily have anything at all to do with what used to be the associated power of bringing paying customers to buy tickets in the cinemas. For every Clint Eastwood who is reliably worth his weight in gold at the box-office there are dozens who, like Elizabeth Taylor, may display their talent in films but save their genius for their very public private lives.

A NOTE ON PHOTOGRAPHERS

Where then does the studio portrait photographer, that mainstay of the Hollywood system in its heyday, fit into this pattern of the developing British film industry? The answer is, much less obviously than might be expected, and quite often not at all. In Hollywood the importance of the fan magazines as a vital (two-way) channel of information and opinion between the film company and its public was already recognized by the beginning of the twenties. The magazines were the obvious way of introducing a new face instantly to a vast public, and since they were always avid for fresh material, it was a very cheap way of publicizing – much cheaper, anyway, than risking a whole movie to launch one newcomer. There was constant feedback, so not only could an absolute beginner be eased painlessly in, with properly planted stories and – most important – alluring portraits, but any contemplated changes could be tested first. Would the public like this dark-haired vamp to become a bubbly, blonde, all-American girl? Would they prefer this male star with or without a moustache? 'Try it and see' was the motto.

Essential to this testing and selling process was the man (or occasionally woman) who took the pictures. Though in smaller film studios the distinctions might have remained a little muzzy, by 1928, when the photographers were unionized, the major studios already had a defined hierarchy: there were the people who took the stills on set, with the performers in action (or more usually quick-frozen, since the training of theatrical photo-calls died hard), and there were those grander beings who had their photographic studios somewhere else in the larger studio complex, and took portraits. The portraits were more or less completely divorced from the film-making process except at the highest level. The two kinds of photographer were even answerable to, or working in collaboration with, different people: the stills photographer with the unit publicist, the portrait photographer with the company head of publicity. And though the portrait might sometimes be directly connected with a movie in production as far as costume and make-up were concerned, essentially it was designed as a thing-in-itself, part of a strategy far longer-term than the promotion of a single movie, part of the year-round process of selling the stars, quite separate from whatever movie they might be triumphing or bombing in at that particular moment.

Now since the British cinema was always organizationally behind the Hollywood times, being a lot poorer and more primitive in most respects – at least until the late forties – it was unlikely that such fine distinctions would be observed, or such long-term master plans laid. Throughout the silent era there hardly existed a star in British films who was not primarily a stage star and who did not consider the cinema an inferior activity occasionally annexed to the main business of living. Betty Balfour was really the only total film star, and Ivor Novello one of the very few who could legitimately be regarded as equally big in both worlds, if the screen did not have a slight advantage. Geographically too, film-making was centred on London, the London of West End theatres and all that went with traditional show-business. What more natural than that whenever some slap-up pictures of film stars were needed they should go where they had always gone: to West End photographers who specialized in society and stage portraiture.

There were many such to choose from. Professional photographers in London belonged to one of three broad categories. There were the studio portraitists, mostly at this stage very conservative and 'painterly' in their presentation of their subjects; there were the news photographers, like James Jarché, who came out of a definitely non-arty tradition of pictorial journalism and gave rise in the next generation to a whole school of more self-conscious 'documentary' photographers like Bill Brandt, Edwin Smith and Humphrey Spender – all of them of course working on location with the raw materials of external reality; and there were the avant-garde experimentalists like Bruguière and, a little later, Moholy-Nagy, who dabbled in surrealism and abstraction. The humble, anonymous stills-photographers employed on the sets of British film studios were closely related to the news photographers; nearly all the portraits that counted were taken by West End portrait photographers, so there was no real need for a special cinematic equivalent; and of course with experiment of any kind the British cinema wanted absolutely no truck.

During the twenties the manner of the portrait photographers was decidedly stately. The dominant figures were Bertram Park, graduate of the famous 'Linked Ring' group in the 1900s, Marcus Adams, who was particularly renowned as a photographer of children, Hugh Cecil who, despite his great success, could hardly wait to give it all up in favour of a rather crazy career as an all-purpose inventor, and Dorothy Wilding. They were all very definitely society photographers, specializing in debs and duchesses and even, if they were lucky, royalty (Hugh Cecil, for example, took the 'accession photograph' of Edward VIII which was the basis for all the short reign's stamps and coins). Of them all, Dorothy Wilding was the one earliest inclined towards show business; she opened her first studio in 1914, moved to Regent Street in 1916 and then became friendly with Hilda Sullivan, who was P. R. person for a number of London theatres. This gave her the entree into theatrical circles, and many of her most memorable images of the twenties and early thirties were of stage stars, some of whom, like Ivor Novello, Evelyn Laye, Jack Buchanan, Gertrude Lawrence, also appeared in films. Though Dorothy Wilding never worked specifically for a film company to produce a group of such portraits, her style showed an appreciation of their individual personalities and added glamour.

In 1923-4 Hugh Cecil took on as an apprentice an eager 18-year-old called Paul Tanqueray, as, ten years later, he would take on another fledgling photographer, Angus McBean. Tanqueray soon broke away and set up on his own, and though naturally he took photographs of anyone who would pay him to do so, he had a particular interest in theatre and the dance, and took many portraits of figures from that world, including a number who later worked in films. He is more relevant to this study than any of his contemporaries because he was the first West End portrait photographer to break away from the painterly tradition of posing and lighting his subjects, and important influences on his style were the Hollywood film close-up and, more particularly, the work of the Hollywood film studio photographers – men like Clarence Sinclair Bull, Russell Ball, Eugene Robert Richee and Otto Dyar – which he saw in American magazines. Even his straight society portraits are subject to this influence, and it is a great pity that he never really had the possibility of carrying this concern for style and a special kind of glamour into British film portrait photography: his assignment in 1939 to make a series of portraits of Wendy Hiller in costume for Gabriel Pascal's film of *Major Barbara* remained an isolated example of working directly in a film context.

During the thirties the film studios became more aware of the importance of the portrait photograph for publicity, especially as a means of attracting the attention of the American public and to encourage audience identification with the stars. Not that, on the whole, they did much about it. Portraits were still normally taken in improvised conditions, on the edge of the film set, by the same photographers who were taking the stills for the film itself. And with a few early exceptions such as Davis Boulton, whose work on films like *King Solomon's Mines* attracted the attention of MGM when they expanded their British studio in 1936, that remained the norm until after the Second World War. But there were signs of change brought on by this awareness. Korda, ever careful of his stars' image, developed a special relationship with the mysterious (but evidently superb) West End photographer Tunbridge, who had a studio in Dover Street at the time when it was as crammed with photographers as Hatton Garden was with diamond merchants. The stills and portraits of Korda's stars from this period having the Tunbridge stamp – Merle Oberon and Leslie Howard in *Scarlet Pimpernel*, Elisabeth Bergner in *Catherine the Great*, all the women in *Private Lives of Don Juan*, Marlene Dietrich and Robert Donat in *Knight Without Armour* – are among the finest and most enduringly beautiful portraits of and since that era.

Michael Balcon and his star director Victor Saville at Gaumont-British also took a more constructive step. When in 1933 they wanted to launch their great star Jessie Matthews on the American market, they understood perfectly well that to do so they would have to use the American method of bombarding the press with portraits of her. Given the importance of these first impressions, it would be necessary to have pictures of a quality comparable with those from American studios. They had already imported a cameraman from Germany to make her happier with her appearance on the screen, and now they brought over the famous American photographer, Otto Dyar, just to revolutionize Jessie Matthews's photographic image. Dyar had made his reputation in the twenties with his pictures of the Brooklyn Bombshell, Clara Bow, and had photographed many other Hollywood stars to glamorous effect. Jessie Matthews was neurotic about her appearance in films: her snub-nose, large lips, weak chin were defects she felt were not apparent on stage but which horrified her when blown up on the screen. The first British portraits of her only added to these misgivings: instead of looking like a wide-eyed doe, she thought she looked like a tadpole. Dyar was brought over to capture in portraits the grace and charm she had when singing and dancing, and add a sheen of glamour. This he did at once by the application of Hollywood knowhow, not only to the posing and lighting, but also to the incidentals like costume, make-up and hair-styling. Having done this he remained in charge of the portrait work at Gaumont-British for three years, and the effect of his presence and his work can be clearly seen if we compare British film portrait photography BD with AD (before and after Dyar).

Davis Boulton on set, *Quo Vadis*, 1950

Sylvia Syms off set, *Expresso Bongo*, 1959

Cornel Lucas pulling into focus a new portrait of his wife, Belinda Lee

James Fox, Cecil Beaton and Mick Jagger off set. *Performance*, 1970

Among the stills cameramen who benefited from this quiet revolution were such fine photographers as Davis Boulton and George Cannons, the latter billed professionally for much of his London studio photographer's career as 'Cannons of Hollywood'. Davis Boulton studied at Bath Art School and went through a photographic apprenticeship before getting his first job in films at the old Fox studios, Wembley, in 1934, when he was 23. From then on he was a stills photographer on set and location with Gaumont-British, with MGM during its late-thirties flirtation with British production on *A Yank at Oxford*, *The Citadel* and *Goodbye Mr Chips*, and with a variety of other companies during and after the war. In 1948 he went back under contract to MGM again, where he remained, until his retirement, in charge of the stills department on their British and European productions such as *Edward My Son, Knights of the Round Table, Quentin Durward, Ben-Hur, Tom Thumb* and *Quo Vadis*. During all this time Boulton was an all-purpose stills photographer of the old school; he never specialized, any more than did most of his contemporaries, in the portrait as such. And yet when he took portraits, as he sometimes did in the course of his general duties on a film, the results could be as memorable as his wonderful Ralph Richardson shown here – making one regret that he did not do it more often.

George Cannons had a more picturesque career. Older than Boulton (he was born in 1897), he went out to Hollywood just after the First World War and made a career as a stills photographer for Mack Sennett and others almost equally unlikely. Unlikely, that is, in relation to what he did when he first came back during the thirties: he set up a portrait studio in the West End under the imposing title 'Cannons of Hollywood', and set out to impart a little Hollywood glamour to a motley collection of dowagers, young marrieds, children and even, on occasion, dogs. By the time the Second World War came he had got fed up with that, and went back to films as a stills photographer under contract to Rank, though he managed somehow to get himself assigned mainly to interesting productions like *Black Narcissus* (Deborah Kerr) and *The Red Shoes* (Moira Shearer), as well as occasional bizarre ones, like *London Town*. And since he had, after all, been a known portrait photographer, it was only natural that though but a stills photographer he should be called on more often than most to do portraits of the stars.

As late as 1951 the idea of having a separate specialist to take portraits in a separate, special place was still generally looked upon askance by British studios. What changed that was one man and his success with one particular assignment. Cornel Lucas was born in 1921 and though an enthusiastic student of photography at the Regent Street Polytechnic he entered the film industry at the age of 16 as a laboratory technician. He soon joined a newsreel team, and during the war served in the photography section of the RAF. In 1946 he went back to films, this time as what he had wanted to be all along, a stills cameraman. He worked for various companies in this capacity, taking portraits along with ordinary film stills, but always in the normal fashion, barely tolerated on the sidelines of the actual shooting. In 1951 he was assigned to the Marlene Dietrich and James Stewart starrer *No Highway*, and during shooting the inevitable moment came when he would have to take portraits of one of the most famous and most photographed faces of the century. To add to his terror he knew that she had not approved of the photographer first assigned to the job. The session took place on a vast disused stage, and to keep things light he put on a radio. Unfortunately as Dietrich marched in with a retinue ranging from make-up men and hairdressers right up to the producer of the picture, the radio started to play 'Colonel Bogey'. Dietrich strode over to it, snapped it off and observed calmly: 'That's not necessary, Mr Lucas.'

It was rapidly apparent that she knew all there was to know about lighting her own face, and the session went off without a further hitch, if frostily. But then Dietrich saw the contacts and went over them literally with a magnifying glass, the retoucher did a good job, and the great lady was generously satisfied. Thereafter, Lucas was able to persuade his employers that a separate, properly equipped portrait studio was not some whimsical luxury but, with the increasing internationalization of British production and the expectations of the stars with Hollywood experience, an absolute necessity. He ran his own portrait studio at Pinewood, where Rank had some forty performers under contract, stars and would-be stars (among them the ravishing Belinda Lee who would become Lucas's wife), and a publicity department constantly crying out for material to keep the magazines and newspapers satisfied. In 1959 he became tired of the contract grind, and left to set up his own portrait studio in London, but film and show-business people as well as the world of fashion continued to make up a large part of his clientele.

Apart from Otto Dyar in the mid-thirties, Cornel Lucas was the first photographer in Britain to run his own portrait studio within a film studio and be able to insist on the clear distinction between stills photography and star portraits, not to mention the men who took them. In that position he was one of the key contributors to the 'look' of most British stars of the fifties, often serving them better than the films for which they were cast and the types they were called on to play. In his portraits, Kay Kendall is the star Hollywood would make a few years later. Lucas was the first and probably also the last, since by the beginning of the sixties the film studio system itself was breaking down, along with all the kinds of continuity it entailed. Almost immediately it became the norm to produce films one at a time, each with its own specially constituted unit, which would certainly include at least one stills photographer but would be unlikely to have room or need for a specialist portrait photographer as well.

In any case, styles in photography as well as styles in stardom were changing. Instead of the preternatural perfection of skin tone and presentation, with never a line or a freckle or a hair out of place, which had been the hallmark of the classic Hollywood portrait photographers, taste swung in the opposite direction: stars were wanted natural-looking (even though it no doubt took a lot of art to get an actor looking natural), and it became the fashion to photograph them unposed, in action, on actual locations, making use of the new high-speed films, portable cameras and tricky wide-angle or telephoto lenses instead of the unmanageable old monsters of studio plate photography. So you couldn't get the same effects; so, you didn't want them. Or not for a while at least – not during Swinging London and kitchen-sink realism and the rough working-class hero, Albert Finney-style, and the independent, mini-skirted Julie Christie striding confidently through our dreams.

There were the new photographers like David Bailey, Clive Arrowsmith, Terry Donovan, Zoe Dominic to cater for this new taste. They might, in very special cases, be hired by the producers to cover a whole film's shooting, but that was unlikely, highly paid and busy as they were. On the other hand, the cinema had ceased to be a world all on its own, with special rules: films might have lost some of their mystique, but now they could be news, in terms the real world understood, as never before. So it was quite likely that a big-time photographer would be hired by a big-time glossy magazine to do a feature on the shooting of a special film or the meteoric progression of a special star, and that the film company would welcome him or her with open arms. Rough, raw reality was supposed to be there for the asking: see the stars sweat and suffer. And if you wanted a touch of old-time glamour and fantasy you could always send in Cecil Beaton or Antony Armstrong-Jones.

It remains true that the magic of a still image can encapsulate more than many whole films ever succeed in doing. How many more people, for instance, remember Skrebneski's elegant, unerotic nude of Vanessa Redgrave, with its immaculately formal disposition of the hair, than can clearly call to mind the film of *Isadora* which inspired it? But now the magic of the movies is observed by outsiders, not distilled in the movie factory itself. Photography as an art-form goes from strength to strength – but the particular, peculiar art of the film portrait photographer is nowadays as much of a museum exhibit as the immovable glass-plate cameras with which so much of it used to be done.

Hollywood star Alice White at work in the gallery doing publicity portraits for *Where There's a Will*, 1936

THE THIRTIES

During the silent era British film stars, or perhaps we should more precisely say leading players, were drawn almost entirely from the stage. Not so much, on the whole, to exploit whatever theatrical following they might have (though most of the theatrical grandees did make at least token appearances on screen), but because the theatre did offer the most convenient source of trained performers, and the cinema, especially after the setback caused by the First World War, had hardly had time to breed its own independent stock. Most of the regular film faces had little standing in the theatre, but they still, in general, acted with inflections derived from stage practice, and all the more noticeably because they were as yet deprived of speech, the principal theatrical vehicle of communication.

With the thirties and the coming of sound there were significant changes, but nothing as radical as might have been expected. As before, the stage was the main source of talent for the screen, though with the coming of speech the screen became rather more attractive, and of course actors who could handle dialogue with aplomb were in ever greater demand. Actors who could handle music and song too, for though the musical never had in the British cinema quite the vogue (or several vogues) it had in Hollywood, it was still popular enough to attract most of the major stars of the flourishing London musical comedy stage: performers like Jack Buchanan, Jack Hulbert and Cicely Courtneidge became almost as regular features in films as in the theatre, and others like Evelyn Laye had at least one or two stabs at screen stardom, both in Britain (*Evensong*) and Hollywood (*The Night Is Young*). Gertrude Lawrence, the bright, particular star of the London stage musical, was oddly enough never really understood and used properly on film, being wasted on inappropriately stuffy roles in films like the classy, lifeless *Rembrandt* or the tushery *Men Are Not Gods*. Perhaps, though, it was she who never properly understood and used her film opportunities.

But the two biggest female stars in British films in the early thirties, Jessie Matthews and Gracie Fields, were both musical stars, both from the theatre, and both were taken at a formative stage and destined to become bigger stars in the cinema than they had ever been in the theatre. There was never any sort of problem about the image Gracie Fields should project: the Lancashire lass from Rochdale had to remain basic, practical and primarily comic or her vast following would begin to suspect she was getting above herself – as they did once or twice when she essayed too heavy a dramatic role, took her singing too seriously for comfort, or tried to play posh and look fancy without a strong element of parody. The publicity pictures of her from her thirties heyday reflect all of this: the look in *Looking on the Bright Side* is not entirely inelegant, but almost ostentatiously lacking in frills and imported glamour.

Jessie Matthews, on the other hand, required more careful visual handling. She was pert and gamine, like a little squirrel, rather than an obvious glamour figure. But she played heroines whose attractions clearly went beyond the tomboy, and, unlike Gracie Fields, who was almost entirely a local, British phenomenon, she was to be exported to the States, where they placed much more store on the glamorous initial impression. One need only compare the attractive but artless image of her recorded by some anonymous studio photographer for

Midshipmaid in 1932 with the exotic confection of plumes and glitter created by Otto Dyar to sell *First a Girl* in 1935, to see the immense difference made by an infusion of Hollywood knowhow. From that point on it is easy to imagine that she would be seriously touted as Ginger Rogers's successor in the arms of Fred Astaire when Ginger went off temporarily to do her own thing, and to feel it was a great pity that contractual difficulties got in the way of her starring with him in *Damsel in Distress*. But that one can so imagine is almost entirely due to this unique foretaste of what Hollywood might have done as shown by Otto Dyar's fine American-style portraits.

Most of the other film star images from the early thirties are nice enough, especially when they offer a straightforward record of people who were already very good-looking, but there is no way that one could guess from Janet Jevons's picture of Flora Robson or a very young Merle Oberon (with cigarette to give maybe a touch of daring sophistication), or Cannons of Hollywood's intense John Loder and the sensationally handsome Jack Buchanan, photographer unknown (both with cigarettes too), that they were in fact film stars rather than peculiarly appealing denizens of the society pages. Margot Grahame by Cannons of Hollywood is a rather different matter, and when only a year or so later than the Jevons portrait of Merle Oberon we come to what Tunbridge did with her in costume for *The Private Life of Don Juan* we know without a doubt that this is show-business.

But here undoubtedly the taste of the man who commissioned the picture comes into play: Korda had a clear idea, not only that he wanted to make stars, but also of what sort of stars they should be. Famously, he turned down Vivien Leigh at first because his complement of female stars was full: Merle Oberon was the exotic (as per Tunbridge), Wendy Barrie was the pure English rose (as seen by Dorothy Wilding), Diana Napier was the 'bitch'. And Vivien Leigh? Well, as Davis Boulton's exquisite portrait for *A Yank at Oxford* in 1938 indicates, she had the potential to be all things to all men and was not to be typed in one particular line.

Even after Otto Dyar had begun to leave his mark on portrait photography in the British cinema, some of the images remain slightly comical: Anna Neagle throwing herself enthusiastically into end-of-term theatricals as Nell Gwynn, defined in terms that a very nice girls' boarding-school might manage to understand, or Elisabeth Bergner with a bad attack of the Middle-European cutes in *Escape Me Never*, do not inspire admiration. But the yearning Lilli Palmer, the spirited, elegantly uncluttered Maureen O'Hara or, above all, Tunbridge's smouldering, sexy portrait of Robert Donat (*Robert Donat?*) with two-thirds of its area boldly occupied with an abstract pattern of light and shade, could easily come out of some major Hollywood portrait studio without incongruity. And there was always one last resource. As the 1938 portrait of Laurence Olivier by Dorothy Wilding unmistakably proves, if you had someone as sensational-looking as that in front of your camera, what did you need with the tricks of art? All you had to do was to take the picture.

HERBERT MARSHALL and EDNA BEST, *The Calendar*, 1931

MERLE OBERON, 1933,
photograph Janet Jevons

JACK BUCHANAN, 1929

FLORA ROBSON, 1931,
photograph Janet Jevons

IDA LUPINO, 1932,
photograph Cannons of Hollywood

WENDY BARRIE, *c.* 1932,
photograph Dorothy Wilding

MARGOT GRAHAME, *c.* 1935,
photograph Cannons of Hollywood

GERTRUDE LAWRENCE, *Candle-Light*, 1929

JOHN LODER, 1934,
photograph Cannons of Hollywood

JESSIE MATTHEWS, *Midshipmaid*, 1932

JOHN GIELGUD, *Good Companions*, 1933

EVELYN LAYE, 1932

ELIZABETH ALLAN, 1932

GRACIE FIELDS, *Looking on the Bright Side*, 1932, photograph A.R.P. Studios

BETTY AMANN, *The Perfect Lady*, 1931

JESSIE MATTHEWS, *First a Girl*, 1935, photograph Otto Dyar

ANNA NEAGLE, *Nell Gwynn*, 1934

NOVA PILBEAM, c. 1937

ELISABETH BERGNER, *Escape Me Never*, 1935

LILLI PALMER, *c.* 1937, photograph Otto Dyar

ROBERT DONAT, 1937, photograph Tunbridge

MERLE OBERON, *The Private Life of Don Juan*, 1934, photograph Tunbridge

BORIS KARLOFF, 1933

MADELEINE CARROLL, c. 1936

ELSA LANCHESTER, *Rembrandt*, 1936, photograph Tunbridge

RALPH RICHARDSON, *The Citadel*, 1938, photograph Davis Boulton

CHARLES LAUGHTON, *The Vessel of Wrath*, 1938

ANNE CRAWFORD, *The Dark Tower*, 1934

GOOGIE WITHERS, *Convict 99*, 1939

LESLIE HOWARD, c. 1939

LAURENCE OLIVIER, 1938, photograph Dorothy Wilding

GREER GARSON, *Goodbye Mr Chips*, 1938, photograph Davis Boulton

MAUREEN O'HARA, 1939

SABU, *The Drum*, 1938

JUNE DUPREZ, *The Thief of Bagdad*, 1940

VIVIEN LEIGH, *A Yank at Oxford*, 1937, photograph Davis Boulton

THE FORTIES

During the war years Jane Russell in *The Outlaw* was not the only person to be mean, moody and magnificent: try James Mason for a start. If any one thing carried him regularly to the top of the male popularity polls in the first half of the decade, it was surely his very clear, consistent star image as the man you love to hate and be loved by. Whole generations of supposedly down-to-earth British women workers on the Home Front apparently asked for nothing better in their dreams than to be slapped around by James Mason, like Margaret Lockwood in *The Man in Grey*, Phyllis Calvert in *Fanny by Gaslight* or Ann Todd in *The Seventh Veil*. At least this meant that British portrait photographers knew very clearly what image they were aiming for with Mason, and it was emphatically not the clean-cut, anyone-for-tennis look.

Nor was there ever any noticeable attempt to present Mason's opposite number, Margaret Lockwood, as a pure English rose. Demure she definitely was not. Ever since the days when Ted Black had spotted in her the qualities that any suburban miss could identify with, she had been cast as a slightly milder British version of the sort of basically common, self-made woman Joan Crawford played so often in Hollywood films of the thirties. Not wise to get on her wrong side; inadvisable to be Phyllis Calvert or Patricia Roc if Lockwood was anywhere in the offing and expect to retain your man – or even, possibly, your life. The low cleavage (historically accurate, we were assured) of her dresses for *The Wicked Lady* did her reputation no harm at all, though it did rather restrict her circle of acquaintance among the American movie-going public, setting the arbiters of the Production Code all of a twitter. But it all made for good, highly coloured black and white pictures for the fan magazines, and the challenge was enthusiastically taken up.

Elsewhere, understated sexuality was the order of the day. Such mid- and late-forties beauties in the British cinema as Sally Gray, Mai Zetterling and Peggy Cummins had to smoulder in a ladylike way, with very little remotely approaching American cheesecake permitted. Even Googie Withers, last glimpsed showing her stocking-tops in the Will Hay extravaganza *Convict 99*, has now become sophisticated and 'mature'. And there were those who made quite a career out of being ladylike on screen and fully, elegantly clad in studio portraits: Deborah Kerr as photographed by Fred Daniels or Joan Greenwood as photographed by John Jay give the general idea. The funniest example of this is the triumphant image of Anna Neagle registered in 1948 for *Spring in Park Lane*. If spirit was the order of the day, no one was going to be more spirited than Anna, and if ladylike was what you wanted, well, just try and find anyone more impeccably elevated than she.

The delights, and dangers, of bringing in an outside photographer of some reputation, which was already occasionally done, are illustrated by Cecil Beaton's portrait of Diana Wynyard in *An Ideal Husband*. The reason he was around is that he had designed the costumes for the film, and clearly he had minimal interest in selling either the picture or the people in it: Diana Wynyard, a true beauty if ever there was one, virtually disappears in yards of elaborate costume which is then outshone by the yet more flowery and ornate rock-garden setting in which she finds herself. A pretty picture indeed, but far removed from your traditional film studio portrait, and not entirely to its own advantage – let alone to the advantage of the film's makers.

Otherwise, the photographers' 'casting' of female stars is eminently conventional. Jean Kent, in Ted Reed's image from *Caravan*, is putting all she has got into being the wild gypsy maiden called for by the role. Valerie Hobson, photographed by Cannons for *The Rocking Horse Winner*, is as always the epitome of upper-class cool. Jean Simmons in 1947 looks both beautiful (she could hardly help doing that), and touchingly vulnerable, a little girl done up in her mother's lipstick. And Christine Norden? Obviously someone in the British cinema had to embody sleaze and provide pin-up interest, so why not this unlikely aberration of Korda's postwar years? Certainly it made a change from the anodyne young ladies turned out by Rank's short-lived charm school at Highbury, run by Molly Terraine in association with the programme of low-budget films at the same studio: few of those ever got anywhere in films, even Rank-financed films, and often publicity photographs are the only evidence of their passage from obscurity to £20-a-week glamour and back to the typing-pool again.

The men in British films during the forties were even easier to pigeonhole. After James Mason departed for Hollywood in 1948 there was no one exactly to take his place. Probably the nearest approach was Anton Walbrook, showing a touch of the old Mason madness as he mistreated Moira Shearer in *The Red Shoes*, and indeed the slightly sadistic ballet impresario Lermontov is the sort of role Mason might have played had he stayed. Otherwise the stars – as opposed to the character actors – were generally either tweedy and reliable or clean-cut and *Boys-Own-Paper*. Trevor Howard around the time of *Brief Encounter* was a sort of Walter Pidgeon with leather elbows on his sports jacket, though later he got crusty instead. Stewart Granger was tall and handsome and always managed to look faintly embarrassed in the silly period outfits he had to wear as another wild gypsy in *Caravan* or as Apollodorus in *Caesar and Cleopatra*. Even the picturesque limp affected by Dennis Price in *The Bad Lord Byron* visibly failed to reconcile this most stylish and elegant of actors to so much fancy-dress folly. As may be observed from the late-forties images of such an unlikely trio of stage-and-screen notables as Noël Coward, Laurence Olivier and Alec Guinness, the true Brit is never happier, on screen or off, than when messing about in well-cut but antique tweed and Viyella. The only wonder is that none of them is smoking a pipe . . .

And then again, there is Vivien Leigh. Some of the best pictures from her *Anna Karenina* were taken by Cecil Beaton, who was once more on the spot as costume designer. The one here is taken by a less famous photographer, Ray Hearne, but it would be hard to better as a portrait which tells you all you need to know about a star and a role, and yet leaves you begging for more. Whatever the ultimate fate of the film, which was by general consent not one of Vivien Leigh's more successful efforts, the magic moment is captured here beyond all criticism. Tolstoy said of his heroine that she was so striking that men and women would stop and look at her in the streets. If she looked in his imagination anything like Vivien Leigh looks here, who could blame them?

ANNA NEAGLE and MICHAEL WILDING, *Spring in Park Lane*, 1948

ROBERT NEWTON, *Major Barbara*, 1941, photograph Davis Boulton

WENDY HILLER, *Major Barbara*, 1941, photograph Davis Boulton

MARGARET LOCKWOOD and JAMES MASON, *The Wicked Lady*, 1944, photograph Ted Reed

JAMES MASON, *The Man in Grey*, 1943,
photograph Ted Reed

PHYLLIS CALVERT, *The Man in Grey*, 1943,
photograph Ted Reed

DENNIS PRICE, *The Bad Lord Byron*, 1949, photograph Norman Hargood

JEAN KENT, *Caravan*, 1946, photograph Ted Reed

JOAN GREENWOOD, *The Bad Lord Byron*, 1949, photograph John Jay

STEWART GRANGER, *Caravan*, 1946, photograph Ted Reed

SALLY GRAY, c. 1945

MAI ZETTERLING, 1949,
photograph John Jay

PATRICIA ROC, 1947,
photograph Ted Reed

TREVOR HOWARD, 1946

DEBORAH KERR, *Black Narcissus*, 1947, photograph Fred Daniels

GOOGIE WITHERS, 1949

JEAN SIMMONS, 1947

MARGARET LOCKWOOD, *I'll Be Your Sweetheart*, 1945, photograph Ted Reed

ANNA NEAGLE, *Spring in Park Lane*, 1948, photograph Davis Boulton

PEGGY CUMMINS, 1948, photograph Ted Reed

CHRISTINE NORDEN, *c.* 1948

PETULA CLARK, *The Huggetts Abroad*, 1949, photograph Cyril Stanborough

JEAN SIMMONS, *Hamlet*, 1948, photograph Wilfrid Newton

DEBORAH KERR, 1948, photograph Davis Boulton

DIANA WYNYARD, *An Ideal Husband*, 1947, photograph Cecil Beaton

NOËL COWARD, 1947

ALEC GUINNESS, 1949

VIVIEN LEIGH, *Anna Karenina*, 1948, photograph Ray Hearne

LAURENCE OLIVIER, 1948, photograph Wilfrid Newton

VALERIE HOBSON, *The Rocking Horse Winner*, 1949, photograph Cannons of Hollywood

ANTON WALBROOK, *The Red Shoes*, 1948

MOIRA SHEARER. *The Red Shoes*, 1948

JEAN SIMMONS, *The Blue Lagoon*, 1948

THE FIFTIES

Bang in the middle of the fifties, John Osborne's angry young hero Jimmy Porter raged in *Look Back in Anger* that there was no trace of a grand design any more: just 'the Brave New Nothing-very-much-thank-you'. It is tempting, if not entirely fair, to apply that specifically to the British film scene. Of course British film-makers and even occasionally British film stars did from time to time have spectacular successes, but as the decade wore on they were increasingly, like David Lean's *The Bridge on the River Kwai* (1957), to be found out of Britain altogether, in the new and impalpable realm of the international super-production. At the other end of the scale there were the deliberately tight-little-island manifestations of the good old British team-spirit, from the heyday of comedy at Balcon's Ealing Studios at the beginning of the decade to the consecration of Carrying On at the end. Admittedly, stars (of a sort) did emerge from these, and far be it from any of us to take Margaret Rutherford or Alastair Sim lightly, comedy being the serious business it is. But they were always star character actors rather than true stars, and so was Alec Guinness until *Kwai* and an Oscar put him in a different category altogether. Up to that point, when publicity portraits were taken they were inevitably in character, because it was only in character that the stars shone with full force: as themselves they were next-to-nobody.

Funnily enough, when it comes down to stars-as-stars, the fifties in Britain were almost exclusively a male preserve. In the forties no one ever complained that there were no meaty roles for female stars, and though interest was fairly evenly balanced between the sexes, it is likely to be the ladies (and not-quite-ladies) we think of first in happy retrospection. But in the fifties who was there? Audrey Hepburn, of course, but then she only became a star in Hollywood, and none of the early British photographs of her gives the slightest hint of her unique quality. Claire Bloom, at a push, but even she did remarkably little on the native British screen. Julie Andrews was around for a while on stage, but it is really cheating even to mention her, since all her fame and all her films find their origin in America. Sylvia Syms, a charming and versatile enough performer, seemed for a few years (about 1956-61) to be getting almost all the female roles that were going, but no one ever really thought of her as a box-office attraction in her own right. And then the divine Kay Kendall flitted all too briefly across our screens in *Genevieve* and *Simon and Laura*, on her way to Hollywood, glamour and a tragically early extinction. But in any case one suspects she was always too much woman for the girl-shy British screen to handle.

Not so the strictly suburban delights of Diana Dors and Joan Collins. They were the light and the dark of it: Dors, busty, bleach-blonde and unashamedly trashy, Collins dark and more discreetly sluttish, wearing (as she later observed) so much mascara she could hardly hold her eyes open. Either or both of them might have played the title role in that apocryphal synthesis *Cosh Girl,* but in the meantime they simmered away, as a rule, in the margins of films which concentrated chiefly on masculine dramas. They were, indeed, the first and last real examples in Britain of that regular Hollywood phenomenon, the star of the pin-ups who never quite makes it to being star of an actual movie. Joan Collins before long took herself off to Hollywood and long years of not quite clinching it on the big screen (she was Esther while look-alike Elizabeth Taylor was Cleopatra) until she finally struck gold with *Dynasty* on the small. As the bitchy, powerful, dominating, glamorous, mascara'd and extravagantly cleavaged Alexis, Collins is a one-woman compendium of all that was most fun and rollicking in the British stars of her childhood. Diana Dors proved (supposedly) that she could act by playing a murderess in *Yield to the Night* (1956); then, at the height of Monroemania, she had her own brief and unsuccessful flirtation with Hollywood, which already has enough blonde bombshells of its own, and came back to be turned into an institution, really just by keeping on keeping on.

But undoubtedly, if you were going to be a star in Britain in the fifties, the thing to be was a man. At the beginning of the period there was suddenly a tremendous, and rather surprising, vogue for Second World War films. Tales of wartime heroism, usually carried out with the stiffest of stiff upper lips, were the order of the day, and in the nature of things it was generally up to our chaps, in the clouds, on (or for that matter under) the high seas, on land and even as prisoners of war, to save the world with a minimum of fuss and bother while their women waited back home for them, dry-eyed and brave as brave could be – and mostly off-screen. All the available male stars were pressed unceremoniously into uniforms of one sort or another, as may be observed from this galaxy of *élégance* more or less *militaire*: Kenneth More in his big hit as the legless flying hero Douglas Bader in *Reach for the Sky*, Michael Redgrave in *The Night My Number Came Up*, Anthony Steel in *Passage Home*, Dirk Bogarde with an *Appointment in London*, and Richard Attenborough in flying jacket for who-knows-what flight of filmic (or merely publicity) fancy. John Mills and Michael Craig, though not strictly military, retain a certain semi-military crispness: even tousled in your actual open air, Michael Craig in *High Tide at Noon* might almost be a Mountie in an off-duty moment.

Norman Gryspeerdt's picture of Michael Craig, incidentally, is in its modest way a pointer towards the shape of things to come. It is quite definitely a portrait, glamour fodder for the fan magazines, rather than a still from the film. And yet it is shot, though at an artistic slant, in the open air, on location, in real sunlight, and is treated in a much more documentary way than stars, even 'rugged' stars, were used to. In the fifties it was exceptional, but by the sixties this would come to be the natural order of things. By the sixties Cornel Lucas had taken himself off into private portrait practice, where as before he could keep all the elements of the photograph under control – the way it was always supposed to be in films. Throughout the fifties, however, he was able to have things pretty much his own way in the film studio, having managed at long last to set up a proper, specialized, full-time portrait studio in Pinewood. The results of his work can be seen here to advantage in the elegant profile of delectable Glynis Johns from *The Card*, the sparkling Kay Kendall from *Simon and Laura*, the unexpectedly sexy Virginia McKenna for *A Town Like Alice* (belying the fact that in films she always played the scrubbed, strongly adorable kind of heroine who never lets any of that sex nonsense get in the way), and perhaps above all the real Hollywood-style glamour image of Belinda Lee, to whom Lucas was at that time married – one of the most spectacular-looking women ever to find a place on the British screen, here presented with the maximum of loving care.

On the whole, though, the portrait photographers in British films were still remarkably square and unadventurous, even when they had such unhackneyed material to deal with as the young Richard Burton in his first film, *Green Grow the Rushes* (1951). Though by the end of the decade Laurence Harvey had allegedly achieved some kind of breakthrough, or breakout, from the gentlemanly ranks of British leading men with his portrayal of Joe Lampton, the ruthlessly climbing working-class hero of *Room at the Top*, Eric Gray's portrait of him, with the new crewcut instead of his old quiff, still plays it safe, with the focus on the Shakespearian actor rather than the rough-and-ready opportunist – who was by all accounts nearer to the real Laurence Harvey. An exception, ready at least occasionally to try something different, odd and even a touch arty, was George Courtney Ward, who introduces some slightly bizarre though maybe appropriate props for his *Sound Barrier* portrait of Ann Todd, produces a quaint 'character' set-up for Ian Carmichael which epitomizes his role in *Simon and Laura* but does not for a moment look like a film still, and manages something really extraordinary for Dirk Bogarde, at that time still a teen-dream on the strength of his *Doctor in the House* light comedy roles, by posing the real (if rather severe-looking) Dirk against a vast blow-up of him in his role as a leather-clad bandit in *The Singer Not the Song*. All of these, though eccentric and imaginative, were still conceived entirely within the established portrait tradition. But with the end of the fifties it was more than time for a change.

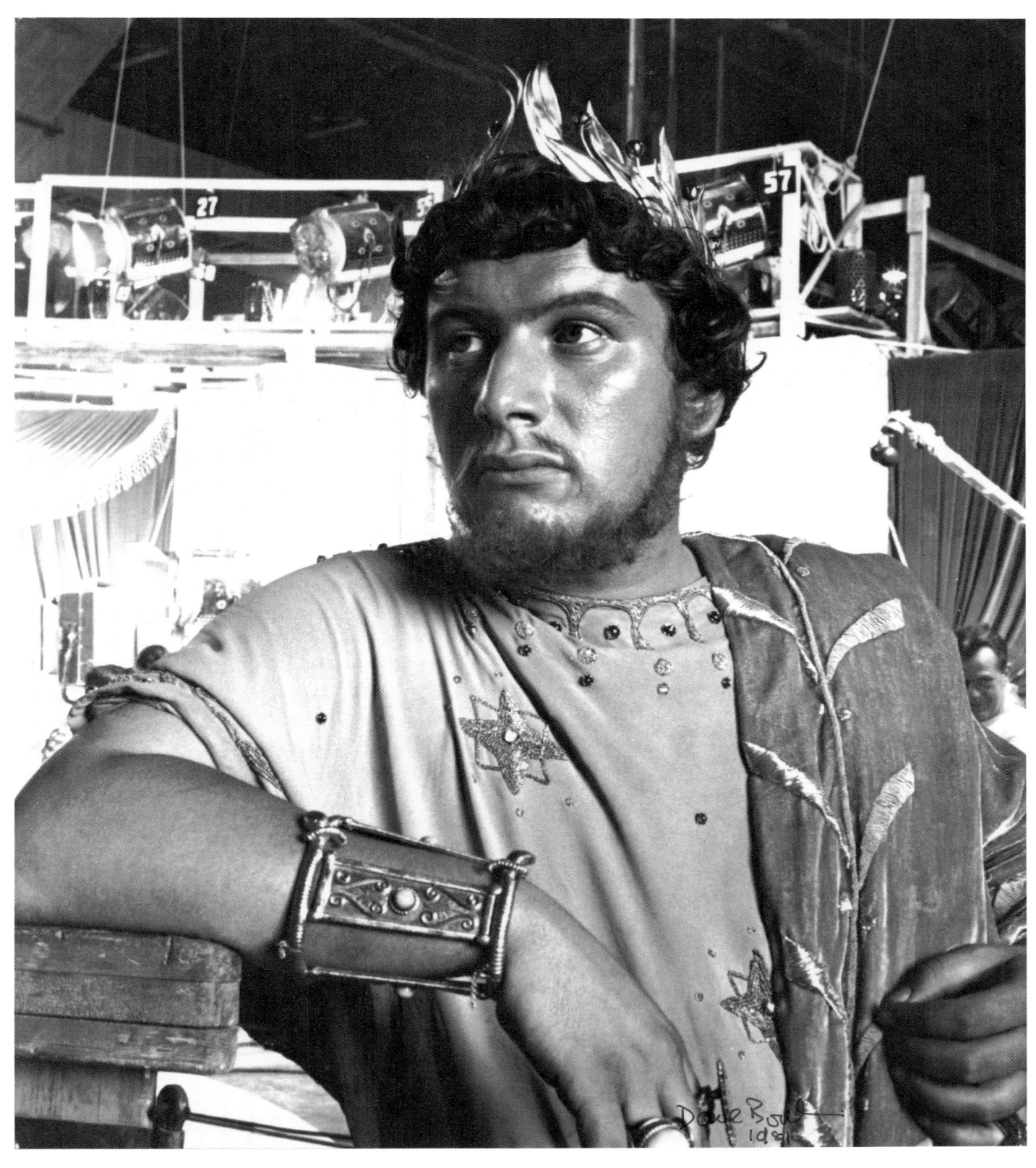

PETER USTINOV, *Quo Vadis*, 1951, photograph Davis Boulton

MARGARET RUTHERFORD, *Innocents in Paris*, 1952

AUDREY HEPBURN, *Laughter in Paradise*, 1951

RICHARD TODD, *The Hasty Heart*, 1949

JULIE ANDREWS, *Cinderella*, 1953, photograph Houston Rogers

CLAIRE BLOOM, *The Man Between*, 1953, photograph Raymond J. Hearne

GLYNIS JOHNS, *The Card*, 1951, photograph Cornel Lucas

MARGARET LEIGHTON, *The Astonished Heart*, 1950, photograph Wilfrid Newton

ALEC GUINNESS, *The Man in a White Suit*, 1951

ANN TODD, *The Sound Barrier*, 1952, photograph George Courtney Ward

JACK HAWKINS, *c.* 1955

KENNETH MORE, *Reach for the Sky*, 1956, photograph Charles Trigg

MICHAEL CRAIG, *High Tide at Noon*, 1957, photograph Norman Gryspeerdt

JOHN MILLS, *c.* 1951

ANTHONY STEELE,
Passage Home, 1955,
photograph Norman Gryspeerdt

MICHAEL REDGRAVE,
The Night My Number Came Up, 1955,
photograph Arthur Evans

DIRK BOGARDE,
Appointment in London, 1953

RICHARD ATTENBOROUGH, 1950,
photograph Charles Trigg

DIANA DORS, 1952, photograph John Jay

TERRY THOMAS, *School for Scoundrels*, 1959

JOAN COLLINS, c. 1952

RICHARD BURTON, *Green Grow the Rushes*, 1951

SYLVIA SYMS, 1957

DINAH SHERIDAN, 1953

KAY KENDALL, *Simon and Laura*, 1955, photograph Cornel Lucas

DAVID NIVEN, c. 1952

IAN CARMICHAEL, *Simon and Laura*, 1955, photograph George Courtney Ward

DIANA DORS, 1955

ALASTAIR SIM, *c.* 1958

REX HARRISON and KAY KENDALL, *The Reluctant Debutante*, 1958

DIRK BOGARDE, 1960, *The Singer Not The Song*, photograph George Courtney Ward

BELINDA LEE, photograph Cornel Lucas

PETER FINCH, *Operation Amsterdam*, 1959, photograph Ian Jeayes

VIRGINIA McKENNA, 1955, photograph Cornel Lucas

LAURENCE HARVEY, *Room at the Top*, 1959, photograph Eric Gray

THE SIXTIES

Contrary to popular belief, the sixties did not start swinging immediately: it was 1964 before Richard Lester got his hands on the Beatles for *A Hard Day's Night* and Beatlemania became a worldwide epidemic; 1965 before *Time* magazine invented 'Swinging London' in a memorable cover-story and, as so often, fact began to ape fiction. Nevertheless, there were signs and portents. The British theatre had been revolutionized (or so it seemed at the time) by a whole influx of new talent. To begin with this was mostly composed of writers, most of them new and young, if not all reliably angry despite the Osborne-derived journalistic tag; then came the directors who directed their plays, and the new breed of actors capable of throwing RADA gentility aside and playing rough working-class types as though they really meant it.

The cinema was, predictably, slower to react. In 1959, three years after the play was originally staged, a rather four-square, tentative film version of *Look Back in Anger* appeared, with everyone concerned trying their best to suggest that John Osborne was really no different from Terence Rattigan. (Time, of course, has proved that he was not after all so very different, but that is another story.) *Room at the Top*, a close contemporary, was based on an angry young novel rather than an angry young play, but the same qualifications apply: the style of the film is glossy and extremely conservative, and established stars – Laurence Harvey and Simone Signoret, in this instance – are used in the traditional star fashion, so that any radical element in the subject is more or less nullified by the way it is presented.

Very shortly a couple of films appeared which did get nearer to the tone and style of the angry new generation, especially since the stars, Albert Finney in *Saturday Night and Sunday Morning* (1960) and Richard Harris in *This Sporting Life* (1963), though presented in very much the old familiar way, did represent a quite obvious break with the refinements of the past. Suddenly everyone was pictured for publicity purposes in grimy industrial backwaters or sitting in gutters, so it really came across that people like Tom Bell and Oliver Reed had working-class origins and took them with becoming seriousness. Not necessarily that they did, when it came to the point of true confessions, but for the time being it was the fashionable image and as many as possible had to conform to it.

So the upper-class accent and the middle-class drama were dead, and life as a result was that much more real and earnest – at least in the movies. Or was it? Oddly enough, no sooner had the new stereotype been established than along came Swinging London, spawned by the never-had-it-so-good era of the Macmillan government. Now it was 'in' again to be a beautiful person, elegantly dressed and even, for the men, a bit of a dandy, living a life of free-spending luxury which had every appearance of being classless, since anyone could look like a lord's son and anybody could claim to be a scion of the working classes, and no one really checked or cared provided you looked the part and had the necessary resources to support it.

The first icons of this age were the Beatles. Simple, unpretentious Liverpool lads catapulted into worldwide super stardom and all that went with it, they embodied the idea of infinite upward mobility while graciously maintaining close contact with their provincial, proletarian roots. A band, even then, on the run, they were not the kind that should or could be photographed formally, and even their studio portrait sessions tended to turn into something mobile and anarchic. They were star performers, but even more, they were NEWS, and were always treated that way by the media. Even in films they were allowed to play only a sanitized, acceptable version of themselves, the fake reality behind the fake fantasy façade. If the real John, Paul, George and Ringo were ever willing to stand up and be recognized, it would certainly not be anywhere near a camera, either movie or portrait.

It was the tone of the times: fantasy still, but fantasy masquerading as and quite possibly mistaking itself for actuality. The new men, if they were not the sublimely classless James Bond, embodied by the stylish but earthy Sean Connery, were either smart and slightly effete, like James Fox and Michael York, or else they were street-wise and capable of handling any social situation, like Michael Caine and Terence Stamp. The girls were either 'real', which meant plain and matter-of-factly sexy, like Rita Tushingham and Glenda Jackson, or dolly birds like Susannah York or Julie Christie or Sarah Miles. Either way they all fitted into the convenient dream-world of the permissive society, where what everyone wanted was within everyone's reach, and the flower children who crowded peaceably (and most likely nude) into rock festivals and love-ins were only the most extreme, and extremely blessed, manifestations of the universal spirit. A pretty picture, even though every *Woodstock* would soon prove to have its dark counterpart in a *Gimme Shelter*, and not every trip engendered by the drug culture turned out to be a pleasant one.

Meanwhile, more portrait photographers continued to make pictures while the sun shone, literally as well as metaphorically. The pictorial styles in vogue mirror the curiously mixed-and-matched style of the period. An appearance of unvarnished reality is in order. Portraits are seldom taken in a conventional studio any more, and when they are, the carefully calculated pose, the immaculate grooming and preternatural perfection that only a really skilled retoucher could impart, are emphatically a thing of the past, relegated with the old hardly moveable 10 × 8 plate cameras in favour of impressions apparently grabbed in a moment with a new portable camera on a new fast film. It is the technique of the reporter on the hop rather than that of the writer polishing his effects at leisure.

But of course, if people supposed that the results of all this were any more truthful – and they did – they were crazy. The camera always lies, or at any rate makes its own truth, and Annette Green's image of a pensive James Fox in the studio or David James's location snapshot of Julie Christie cooling her heels in the shallows are just as fanciful, just as invented as anything produced by Otto Dyar in the thirties or Cornel Lucas in the fifties. What then seemed like an abandonment of convention is now recognizable as the substitution of another convention, different in its surface qualities but ultimately the same in spirit. Stardom is something that happens between the human subject and the camera lens, in the twinkling of a shutter, and any other order of reality has precious little to do with it, in the sixties or ever.

GEORGE HARRISON, RINGO STARR, PAUL McCARTNEY, JOHN LENNON
off set, *A Hard Day's Night*, 1964

RITA TUSHINGHAM, *The Knack*, 1965

PETER COOK and DUDLEY MOORE, *The Wrong Box*, 1967

SEAN CONNERY, 1963

PETER O'TOOLE, 1962

JOHN HURT, 1964

ALBERT FINNEY, *Tom Jones*, 1963, photograph Sandra Lousada

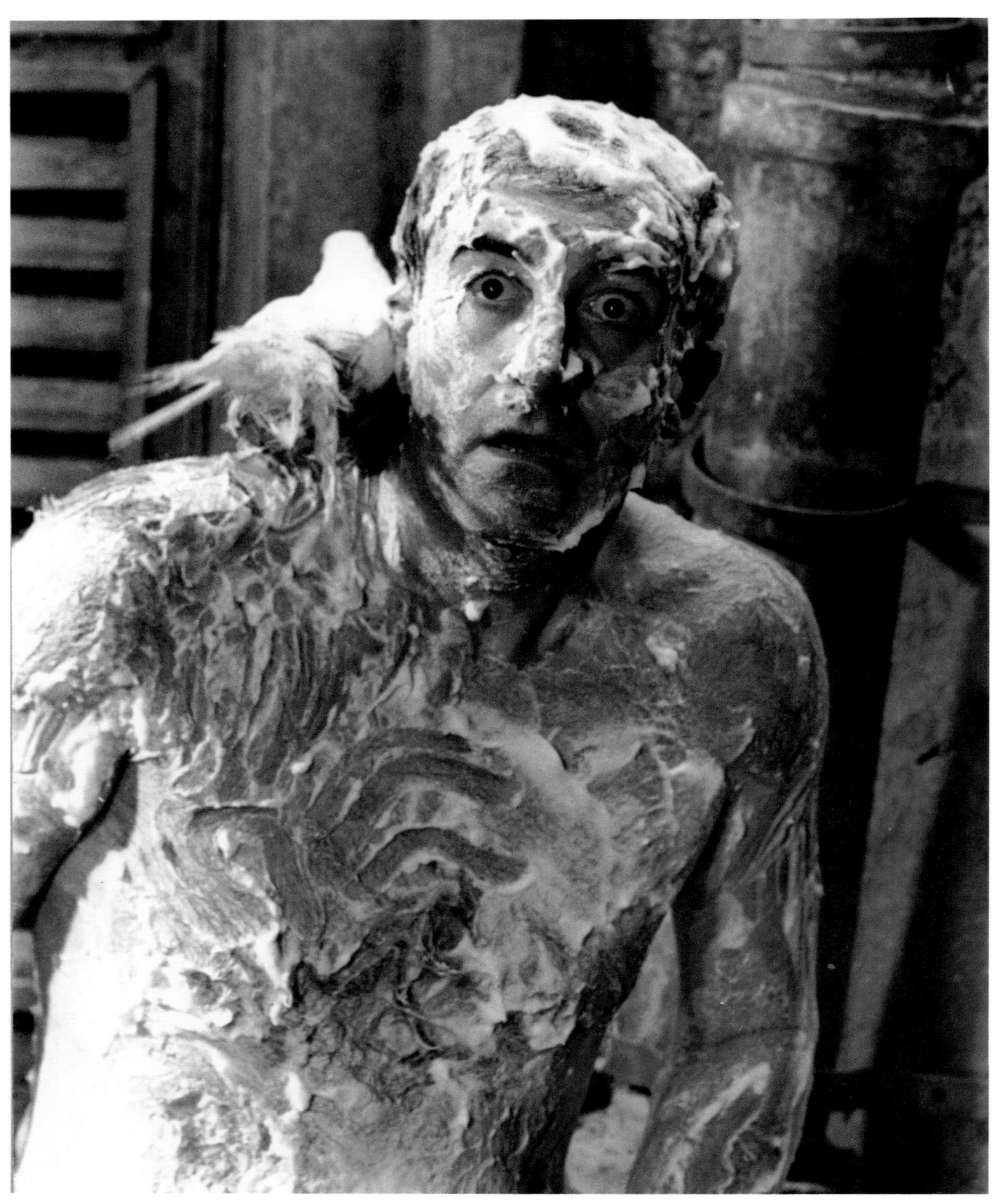

PETER SELLERS, *After the Fox*, 1966

SUSANNAH YORK, *Duffy*, 1968

JULIE CHRISTIE, *The Fast Lady*, 1962,
photograph David James

HAYLEY MILLS, *The Moon-Spinners*, 1964

SARAH MILES, *I Was Happy Here*, 1966

ALAN BATES, 1966

GLENDA JACKSON, *Women in Love*, 1969, photograph David James

MICHAEL YORK, 1967

RICHARD HARRIS, c. 1961

OLIVER REED, c. 1962,
photograph Eric Wilkins

TOM BELL, 1962

JAMES FOX, *Isadora*, 1968, photograph Annette Green

MICHAEL CAINE, *Deadfall*, 1968

TERENCE STAMP, 1961

VANESSA REDGRAVE, *Morgan*, 1966, photograph Patrick Lichfield

JULIE CHRISTIE, *c.* 1967

STANLEY BAKER, *Where's Jack?* 1969

MAGGIE SMITH, *c.* 1967, photograph John Young

SEAN CONNERY, *From Russia With Love*, 1963

MODERN TIMES

So how about, yes how about, today? They had faces then. Who wants moving, who wants true? It's not the screens that have got bigger, it's the people that have got smaller. To mention but a handful of classic formulations of the eternal gripes. Closer to the point, perhaps: things aren't what they used to be – but then they never were. The stars of today are no doubt as interesting, as magnetic, as extraordinary-looking as they ever were. It is just the circumstances and the definition of stardom which have changed. David Bowie may look, in certain lights, very like Ivor Novello, but he could never be the same sort of star – not so much because he is different, but because the world is. The old definitions of movie stardom did not exist in a vacuum, pointing to some external verity; it was all a part of the studio contract system, the way films were produced and distributed, the way players were presented and represented to the public for their approval or disapproval. Without all that, a star in the original sense cannot exist. There will still be those who attract a special, personal sort of devotion, and there will still be those whose pictures we like to have around us. Stars in that sense, yes. *C'est magnifique, mais ce n'est pas la guerre*, or at any rate not the war our fathers fought and sometimes won.

The main problem with this kind of stardom is that it lacks stereotypes. Stereotyping is supposed to be bad, but good or bad, most people's lives, their personal and career decisions are based on stereotypes, with only the occasional break-out into total individuality and originality. This has always been true of stars and the way they were packaged – witness Korda's exotic/English rose/bitch pattern – and the whole star-making process, studio portraits not least, was geared to establishing expectations or very gently modifying them, making the stars something bigger and more general in application than they could ever actually be in life, so that they could be the passive receptacle for as many different dreams as possible. How do you do that when there is little or no continuity or long-term strategy, and either no real models or a plethora, depending on which way you look at it?

The problem is obvious when you look at the star portraits of the seventies and eighties. At most a star may have a particular look promoted for a particular film: the still, fast-fading Swinging Sixties look of Roger Moore as James Bond, the presentation of Helen Mirren in *Hussy* as a witty pastiche (if you recognize the original) of André Kertesz's well-known mid-twenties photograph 'Satiric Dancer'. Which is fine for one film or one role, but means that Helen Mirren, for example, though she has now starred in a number of films, does not have in any way a single, immediately recognizable star image: indeed, you could be forgiven for not even recognizing her as the same person from film to film.

No models or a plethora. There are few current models today anywhere in the film world, and only a few who stick around long enough in the pop world to become role models. On the other hand, the whole of film history and the whole history of photography are laid out before the devisers of the star portrait today, and reference or out-and-out pastiche have become the done thing. The famous profile photograph of David Bowie done for *The Man Who Fell to Earth* was deliberately modelled on a classic of Ivor Novello. The silly picture here of that great modern beauty Charlotte Rampling, clutching a toy tiger to her discreetly concealed bosom, looks less like a serious pin-up than a homage to the pin-up photographers of the fifties. It is as though the stars today are like the recent crop of Hollywood tycoons, not so much representing themselves as playing at being their predecessors, or living out their own fantasy images of what their predecessors ought to have been. There is a vital difference here, one that the camera picks up unerringly: Marilyn Monroe just wanted to be Marilyn Monroe, superstar to the nth degree; Harry Cohn (presumably) had most of his energies taken up with just being Harry Cohn, running a studio, bedding starlets, making movies. But what are we to make of the stars today who want to be Marilyn Monroe, the tycoons who want to be Harry Cohn, who live all their lives as reflections of the past? More important, what is the camera to make of them?

But every situation has its compensations. After all, if you are harking back to the thirties or forties conception of stardom, one of the most obvious and potent ways of doing so is to hark back also to the way Hollywood presented stars to the millions of breathless fans. So glamorous studio portraits are back, and though not so many 8 × 10 cameras have been wheeled out from whatever photographic museums they are hiding in, all that can be done by lighting, make-up and atmosphere to reproduce their effects is being done again. The revival really began around the time Keith Carradine, fresh from his triumph in *Nashville*, decided that he would like none other than George Hurrell, then well into his seventies, to do the portraits for his new album cover, just because he liked the effect of Hurrell's thirties pictures and wanted him to re-create it.

Photographers being on the whole a long-lived breed, Hurrell is not the only one of the classic generation still around, still active. And it seems appropriate that this book should end with a stunning portrait of a young British star of the sixties, Jane Asher, by a Hollywood great, Laszlo Willinger, actually taken in the eighties. It shows all the magic that so much contemporary portrait photography has lost. It also has the advantage, remarkably enough, of making a completely fresh statement. Willinger does not try to make Jane Asher into another Ingrid Bergman, or Joan Crawford, or Hedy Lamarr, or Vivien Leigh, or any of the other famous beauties he photographed in their heyday. Instead he makes her into the first and only Jane Asher, purified and perfected by the photographer's considered art. It takes a rare talent these days to do that, but when it is done right the thrill is unique and irreplaceable: the time, the place and the loved one all come together and we are left to warm ourselves in the heat of their fusion, to light our way with the billion candlepower of genuine starlight.

ROGER MOORE, *The Man With the Golden Gun*, 1974

CHARLOTTE RAMPLING, 1974

DAVID ESSEX, c. 1973

HELEN MIRREN, *Hussy*, 1979

JACQUELINE BISSET, *c.* 1970, photograph Clifford Kent

STING, *c.* 1979

DAVID BOWIE, 1983

ALICE KRIGE, *Ghost Story*, 1981

JOAN COLLINS, 1982

JEREMY IRONS, 1980

TOM CONTI, *Eclipse*, 1976

RUPERT EVERETT, *Another Country*, 1984

JANE ASHER, 1983, photograph Laszlo Willinger

LIST OF STARS

(Page numbers refer to plates)

Allan, Elizabeth 37
Amann, Betty 39
Andrews, Julie 97
Asher, Jane 159
Attenborough, Richard 105
Baker, Stanley 142
Balfour, Betty 12
Barrie, Wendy 33
Bates, Alan 134
Bell, Tom 136
Bergner, Elisabeth 43
Best, Edna 31
Bisset, Jacqueline 151
Bloom, Claire 98
Bogarde, Dirk 105, 118
Bowie, David 153
Brook, Clive 13
Buchanan, Jack 32
Burton, Richard 109
Caine, Michael 138
Calvert, Phyllis 67
Carmichael, Ian 114
Carroll, Madeleine 48
Christie, Julie 133, 141
Clark, Petula 78
Collins, Joan 108, 155
Colman, Ronald 13
Connery, Sean 128, 144
Conti, Tom 157
Cook, Peter 127
Coward. Noël 82
Craig, Michael 104
Crawford, Ann 52
Cummins, Peggy 76
Donat, Robert 45
Dors, Diana 106, 115
Duprez, June 59
Essex, David 149
Everett, Rupert 158
Fields, Gracie 38
Finch, Peter 120
Finney, Albert 131
Fox, James 137
Garson, Greer 56
Gielgud, John 35

Grahame, Margot 33
Granger, Stewart 71
Gray, Sally 72
Greenwood, Joan 70
Guinness, Alec 83, 101
Harris, Richard 136
Harrison, George 125
Harrison, Rex 117
Harvey, Laurence 122
Hawkins, Jack 103
Hepburn, Audrey 95
Hiller, Wendy 65
Hobson, Valerie 86
Howard, Leslie 54
Howard, Trevor 73
Hurt, John 130
Irons, Jeremy 156
Jackson, Glenda 135
Johns, Glynis 99
Karloff, Boris 47
Kendall, Kay 112, 117
Kent, Jean 69
Kerr, Deborah 73, 80
Krige, Alice 154
Lanchester, Elsa 49
Laughton, Charles 51
Lawrence, Gertrude 33
Laye, Evelyn 36
Lee, Belinda 119
Leigh, Vivien 60, 84
Leighton, Margaret 100
Lennon, John 125
Lockwood, Margaret 66, 74
Loder, John 33
Lupino, Ida 32
McCartney, Paul 125
McKenna, Virginia 121
Marshall, Herbert 31
Mason, James 66, 67
Matthews, Jessie 34, 40
Miles, Sarah 133
Mills, Hayley 133
Mills, John 104
Mirren, Helen 150
Moore, Dudley 127
Moore, Roger 147

More, Kenneth 104
Neagle, Anna 41, 63, 75
Newton, Robert 64
Niven, David 113
Norden, Christine 77
Novello, Ivor 7
Oberon, Merle 32, 46
O'Hara, Maureen 57
Olivier, Laurence 55, 85
O'Toole, Peter 129
Palmer, Lilli 44
Pilbeam, Nova 42
Poulton, Mabel 12
Price, Dennis 68
Rampling, Charlotte 148
Redgrave, Michael 105
Redgrave, Vanessa 140
Reed, Oliver 136
Richardson, Ralph 50
Robson, Flora 32
Roc, Patricia 72
Rutherford, Margaret 94
Sabu 58
Sellers, Peter 132
Shearer, Moira 88
Sheridan, Dinah 111
Sim, Alastair 116
Simmons, Jean 73, 79, 89
Smith, Maggie 143
Stamp, Terence 139
Starr, Ringo 125
Steele, Anthony 105
Sting 152
Syms, Sylvia 110
Thomas, Terry 107
Todd, Ann 102
Todd, Richard 96
Tushingham, Rita 126
Ustinov, Peter 93
Walbrook, Anton 87
Wilding, Michael 63
Withers, Googie 53, 73
Wynyard, Diana 81
York, Michael 136
York, Susannah 133
Zetterling, Mai 72